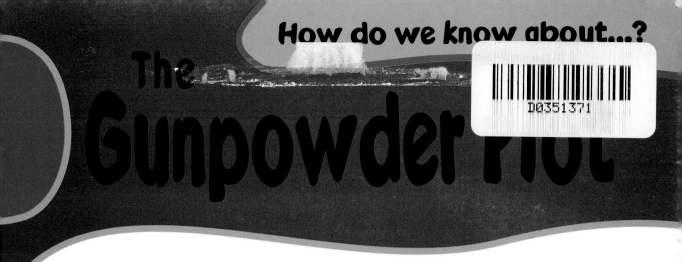

# The Gunpowder Plot

Deborah Fox

www.heinemann.co.uk/library
Visit our website to find out more information about Heinemann Library books.

To order:
 Phone 44 (0) 1865 888066
 Send a fax to 44 (0) 1865 314091
 Visit the Heinemann Bookshop at www.heinemann.co.uk/library to browse our catalogue and order online.

First published in Great Britain by Heinemann Library, Halley Court, Jordan Hill, Oxford OX2 8EJ, a division of Reed Educational and Professional Publishing Ltd. Heinemann is a registered trademark of Reed Educational & Professional Publishing Ltd.

OXFORD  MELBOURNE  AUCKLAND  JOHANNESBURG  BLANTYRE
GABORONE  IBADAN  PORTSMOUTH (NH) USA  CHICAGO

Designed by Joanna Hinton-Malivoire
Illustrations by Peter Bull Art Studio
Originated by Repro Multi Warna
Printed by South China Printing Company China

10 digit ISBN 0 431 12330 6    (hardback)
13 digit ISBN 978 0 431 12330 1 ( hardback )

07 06 05 04 03
10 9 8 7 6 5 4 3 2 1

10 digit ISBN 0 431 12336 5 ( Paperback )
13 digit ISBN 978 0 431 12336 3 ( Paperback )

10 09 08
10 9 8 7 6 5 4

**British Library Cataloguing in Publication Data**
Fox, Deborah
How do we know about the Gunpowder Plot?
1.Gunpowder Plot, 1605 - Juvenile literature
I.Title II.The Gunpowder Plot
942'.061

**Acknowledgements**
The Publishers would like to thank the following for permission to reproduce photographs: Andy Williams: p27; Cambridge University Library: p21; Collections: p5; Fotomas: p24; Mary Evans Picture Library: pp22, 23; PA Photos: p26; Public Record Office: pp21, 25.

Cover photograph reproduced with permission of Mary Evans Picture Library.

Words printed in **bold letters like these** are explained in the Glossary

# Contents

# Remember, remember

'Remember, remember the fifth of November,
Gunpowder, **treason** and plot.
I see no reason why gunpowder treason
Should ever be forgot.'

Have you heard this rhyme before?

Do you know why we have bonfires and fireworks on 5 November? Have you ever wondered why we put a 'guy' on the flames? This book tells the story of the gunpowder plot.

# The plan

In 1605, England was ruled by King James I. He was a **Protestant**. James was worried that the **Catholics** would try to stop him being King, so he punished Catholics who **worshipped**.

Catholics in England were very unhappy. One, called Robert Catesby, thought of a plan to get rid of the King. He met with other Catholics to talk about what they could do.

# Kill the King

Robert Catesby said that they could kill King James and his family by blowing up the **Houses of Parliament** on the opening day of Parliament.

The King, his wife and his eldest son
would all be there for the Opening of
Parliament on 5 November.

# Guy Fawkes

The plotters needed someone who knew about gunpowder. One of them, Thomas Wintour, had heard about a **Catholic** called Guy Fawkes. Guy was an **expert** with gunpowder.

Guy was in Europe fighting for King Philip of Spain who was Catholic too. Thomas met Guy and persuaded him to return to England and join the plot.

# Digging the tunnel

One of the plotters rented a house near **Parliament**. His plan was to dig a **tunnel** underneath Parliament and blow it up. The plotters started to dig, but it took far too long.

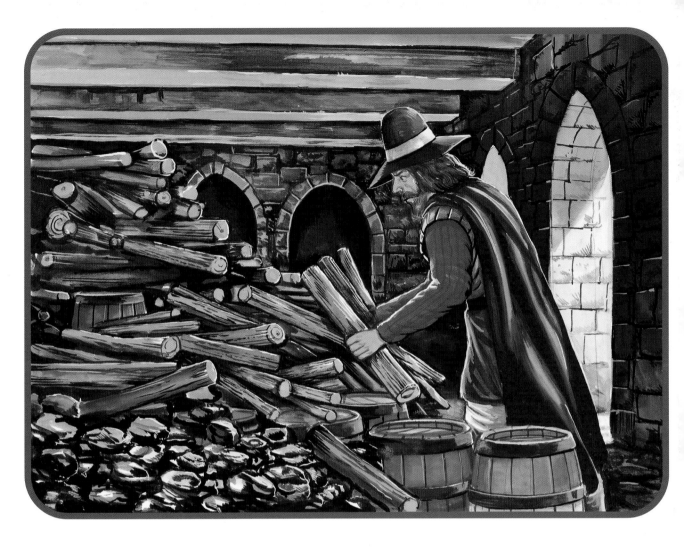

Then they discovered that they could rent a **cellar** underneath Parliament. There they stored 36 barrels of gunpowder, carefully hidden under a pile of coal and firewood.

# The letter

On 26 October 1605, a servant handed a letter to his master, Lord Monteagle. The letter warned the **Catholic** Lord to stay away from the Opening of **Parliament** on 5 November.

Lord Monteagle was worried. He showed the letter to the Earl of Salisbury, who worked closely with King James. The Earl took the letter to the King.

# Too late!

On 4 November 1605, the King ordered that **Parliament** be searched. In the **cellars** they found a dark figure crouching next to the gunpowder. Guy was ready to light the **fuse**. Too late!

On 5 November 1605, people in London celebrated the discovery of the plot by lighting bonfires. In 1806, people started throwing a model of Guy Fawkes on to the flames.

# The trial

Guy was taken to the **Tower of London**. He refused to name the other plotters. But, after days of **torture**, Guy was very weak, and he **confessed**.

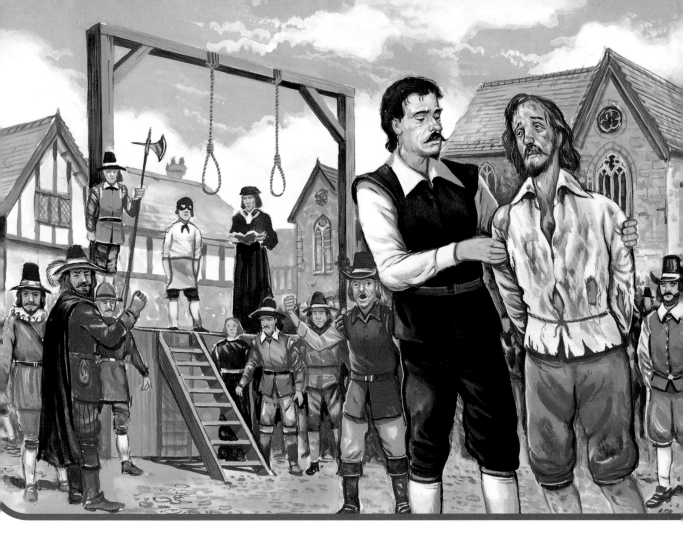

The plotters had to get away fast, but the King's men caught them. Robert and three others were wounded and later died. At their trial, the plotters were charged with **treason** and sentenced to death.

# How do we know?

After Guy and the other plotters had been killed, all the details of the plot were written down in a book called *The King's Book*. This is a photograph of it.

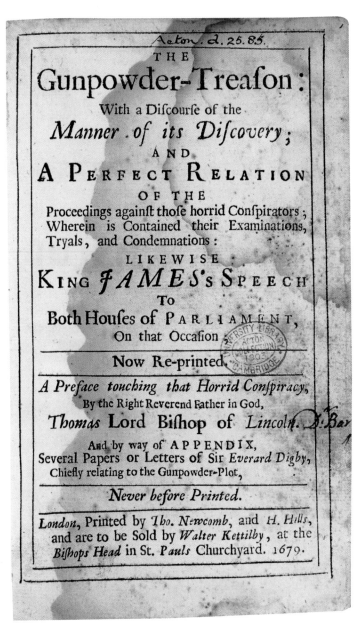

This is a photograph of the letter sent to Lord Monteagle warning him not to go to the Opening of **Parliament**.

# Pictures and objects

Artists drew pictures of the story of the Gunpowder Plot. This picture has been **engraved**. It shows eight of the thirteen plotters.

This lantern is said to have belonged to Guy Fawkes. Perhaps he used it in the dark **cellars**?

# Was Guy Fawkes tortured?

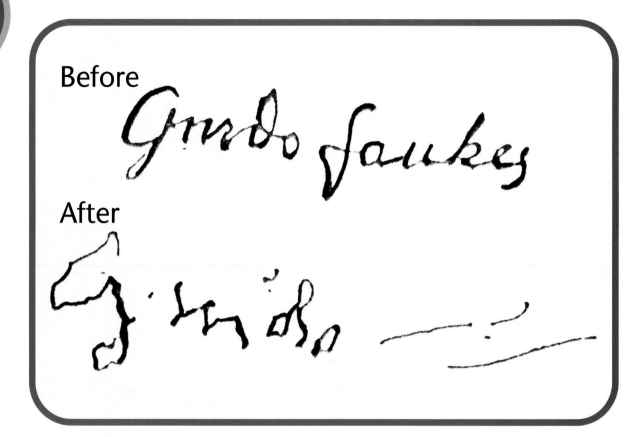

Before

After

Here is Guy's **signature** before and after he was **tortured**. Look how wobbly his name is after being tortured (he called himself Guido). He was very weak.

This letter is signed by King James I.
It gives his permission for Guy to
be tortured.

# Famous places

Every year the **cellars** where Guy was found are searched – not because anyone thinks gunpowder is there, but to remember the event.

The plotters who fled agreed to meet at the Old Red Lion Inn in Dunchurch, Warwickshire. The Inn is now known as Guy Fawkes' House. This is a photograph of how it looks today.

# Timeline

*1603* James I becomes King of England.

*20 May 1604* Plotters meet to discuss their plan.

*1604* Plotters rent a house near the **Houses of Parliament** and they start to dig a **tunnel**.

*25 March 1605* A **cellar** under the Houses of Parliament becomes empty and Thomas Percy, one of the plotters, rents it.

*26 October 1605* Lord Monteagle receives a letter warning him to stay away from the Opening of Parliament.

*1 November 1605* King James I is shown the letter.

*4 November 1605* Guy Fawkes hides in the cellar ready to light the **fuse**, but he is caught.

*5 November 1605* The people celebrate by lighting bonfires in the streets.

*27 January 1606* The trial of the plotters.

*31 January 1606* The plotters are **executed**.

# Biographies

## Guy Fawkes

Guy Fawkes was born in York in 1570. He was born a **Protestant** but later became a **Catholic** because his new stepfather was Catholic. Guy fought for the Spanish King Philip in 1596 and became an **expert** in using gunpowder. He was executed on 31 January 1606 for his part in the Gunpowder Plot.

## Robert Catesby

Robert Catesby was born in 1573. His father died in 1598 and soon after his mother died too. For the rest of his life Robert was dedicated to the Catholic faith. He was the leader of the Gunpowder Plot. On 8 November 1605, after a fight with the King's soldiers, he was wounded and died.

# Glossary

**Catholic**  a Christian who belongs to the Roman Catholic Church. The Pope is the Head of this Church.

**cellar**  an underground room or area, usually where things are stored

**confess**  to admit something; to say that something is true

**engraved**  written or drawn onto a block of material that can be printed

**executed**  killed as a punishment

**expert**  a person who knows a lot about a subject

**fuse**  the part that is lit to set off an explosive

**Houses of Parliament**  the place where laws are made in Britain. There are two Houses – the House of Commons and the House of Lords.

**Protestant**  a Christian who does not belong to the Roman Catholic Church. Protestants separated from the Catholic Church many years ago to set up their own Church.

**signature** when people sign letters they write their names in their own special way

**torture** to cause someone pain usually in order to gain information

**Tower of London** a prison in London. It is now a Museum.

**treason** when someone speaks out or does something against the good of the country or the King or Queen

**tunnel** an underground passage

**worship** to show respect and love for a god

# Further reading

*Don't Forget: Bonfire Night*, Monica Hughes, Heinemann Library, 2002

*Great Events: The Gunpowder Plot*, Gillian Clements, Franklin Watts, 2001

*Lives and Times: Guy Fawkes*, Rachael Bell, Heinemann Library, 1998

# Index